W9-BLT-245

How *Rent* Made It to the Stage

George Capaccio

Cavendish Square

New York

Published in 2019 by Cavendish Square Publishing, LLC
243 5th Avenue, Suite 136, New York, NY 10016
Copyright © 2019 by Cavendish Square Publishing, LLC

First Edition

Library of Congress Cataloging-in-Publication Data

Names: Capaccio, George, author.
Title: How Rent made it to the stage / George Capaccio.
Description: New York : Cavendish Square, 2019. | Series: Getting to Broadway | Includes
bibliographical references and index. | Audience: Grades 7-12.
Identifiers: LCCN 2017052802 (print) | LCCN 2017053451 (ebook) | ISBN
9781502635112 (library bound) | ISBN 9781502635136 (pbk.) | ISBN
9781502635129 (ebook)
Subjects: LCSH: Larson, Jonathan. Rent--Juvenile literature.
Classification: LCC ML3930.L177 (ebook) | LCC ML3930.L177 C37 2018 (print) |
DDC 792.6/42--dc23
LC record available at https://lccn.loc.gov/2017052802

Editorial Director: David McNamara
Editor: Tracey Maciejewski
Copy Editor: Rebecca Rohan
Associate Art Director: Amy Greenan
Designer: Lindsey Auten
Production Coordinator: Karol Szymczuk
Photo Research: J8 Media

The photographs in this book are used by permission and through the courtesy of: Cover
Theatrepix/Alamy Stock Photo; p. 4 Alex Segre/Alamy Stock Photo; p. 12 Adoc Photos/
Corbis/Getty Images; p. 14 Hulton Archive/Getty Images; p. 16 Bettina Cirone/Science
Source/Getty Images; p. 20 Chronicle/Alamy Stock Photo; p. 23, 26, 29 John Snelling/Getty
Images; p. 25 De Agostini/A. Dagli Orti/Getty Images; p. 30 Mark Mainz/Getty Images;
p. 31, 33 Walter McBride/Getty Images; p. 36 Mireya Acierto/Getty Images; p. 38, 39, 64
Carol Rosegg/Broadway Across America/Getty Images; p. 48 Gil C/Shutterstock.com; p.
52 Richard Levine/Alamy Stock Photo; p. 54 Richard Drew/AP Images; p. 57 Fresh photos
from all over the worls/Moment/Getty Images; p. 59 Mitchell Funk/Photographer's Choice/
Getty Images; p. 61 Catherine McGann/Getty Images; p. 63 Bruce Glikas/FilmMagic/Getty
Images; p. 67 Theo Wargo/Getty Images; p. 74 Janette Pellegrini/WireImage/Getty Images;
p. 77 Hank Walker/The LIFE Picture Collection/Getty Images; p. 80 Jason Kempin/Wire-
Image/Getty Images; p. 83 Paul Hawthorne/Getty Images.
Printed in the United States of America

Contents

Chapter 1

Life in Bohemia

Have you ever dreamed of becoming an artist? Do you wonder if you have the necessary talent to succeed as a musician, a writer, or an actor? And if you were to pursue this dream, what sort of life do you imagine yourself living?

No Bed of Roses

The Broadway musical *Rent* celebrates the lives of young, struggling artists living in New York City's East Village, a neighborhood known for its creative community—in addition to generations of immigrant groups, including Germans and Irish in the early 1900s and Eastern European Jews followed by Puerto Ricans in the second half of the twentieth century.

Opposite: New York City's East Village has a thriving artistic community and a variety of unique shops and services.

Now, the neighborhood is changing, becoming more gentrified, but in the late 1980s, the East Village had plenty of crumbling, rundown buildings where poor artists could find cheap spaces in which to live and create their art. Roger and Mark, two of the main characters in *Rent*, are roommates sharing a grungy apartment in the East Village. Before being converted into apartments, the building in which they live had been a factory. Benny, the owner of the building and Roger and Mark's landlord, used to be their good friend and roommate. But those days are long gone. Benny married a woman from a well-to-do family and has abandoned the nonconformist values they once shared. Benny, in other words, has "sold out." He is no longer a bohemian like his former friends.

Roger is a documentary filmmaker. His latest project is making an unscripted movie about his friends. His roommate Mark is a musician. Both young men are barely able to make ends meet and have fallen way behind in their rent. When the play begins, they are cold and hungry. It's Christmas Eve, 1989, and their apartment has no heat and their cupboards are bare since they don't have enough money between them to buy groceries. As if this weren't bad enough, Roger has AIDS and doesn't expect to live much longer.

In the time he has left, his central ambition is to create one truly memorable song that will serve as his lasting legacy and give his life the meaning and purpose he feels it lacks. Roger is also a recovering heroin addict. His former girlfriend, Julie, committed suicide by slitting her wrists after discovering that she too had AIDS, possibly from the two of them sharing contaminated needles when using heroin.

Despite the difficulties Mark and Roger are facing, they are not about to give up their dreams and move to a pleasant neighborhood in suburbia. And the musical *Rent* is anything but tragic. Like its creator, Jonathan Larson, it's brimming with optimism and youthful energy. *Rent* celebrates life, friendship, creativity, and love in all its guises and manifestations. Unlike most Broadway shows at the time of *Rent*'s debut, it features nonstereotypical gay, lesbian, and transvestite characters along with heterosexual ones. The successive casts of *Rent* have all been multiracial and multiethnic; with few exceptions, the characters they play are poor or working class, another dramatic departure from typical Broadway fare.

Jonathan Larson, Composer and Game Changer

Rent is a rock opera. Jonathan Larson, who wrote the book, composed the music, and wrote the lyrics, knew a great deal about musical theater. Only thirty-five at the time of *Rent*'s move from Off-Broadway's New York Theatre Workshop to the Nederlander Theatre on Broadway, Larson had been a longtime fan and serious student of more traditional musicals like *Miss Saigon*, *The Phantom of the Opera*, and *Les Misérables*. His dream was to create a work in which rock music would really stand out in all its rawness and power. Larson felt that in most shows featuring rock music, the music was watered down, deprived of its natural, high-octane energy in order to appeal to the patrons of Broadway shows, who tended to be older and more conservative.

What about members of the younger generation who couldn't afford the price of a ticket to a Broadway show or who were turned off by the apparent irrelevance of such shows—irrelevant in the sense that these shows didn't address their most immediate concerns? Young people in the 1980s and '90s had grown up watching music videos on MTV in which the music was anything but diluted. According to Larson's former collaborator, Billy Aronson, Larson had once said to him, "I've been waiting for a chance to bring the MTV generation … to the theatre. Nobody goes to the theatre who likes MTV or who likes rock music, and we have to change that …"

Larson wanted *Rent* to be the *Hair* of the '90s. *Hair* was a seminal musical of the 1960s and '70s that spoke to the counterculture generation, the baby boomers who had rejected the bourgeois values of their parents and wanted to create an alternative society in which love was the guiding principle and dog-eat-dog capitalism was replaced by life in community. The rock music of *Hair* was the real thing and not the soft pop rock that was then so current in shows that billed themselves as rock musicals or rock operas. But would a rock score do justice to the material Larson was working with? Would he have to water it down in order to make it work? Not if he could help it. After all, the musical *Hair* had become an international hit. Could the same thing be done with *Rent*?

Theoretically, rock shouldn't work in musical theater. The lyrics in this form of theater have a lot of heavy lifting to do, especially if the musical is sung-through with little or no dialogue. In that case, song lyrics are tasked with telling the story and revealing character, and they have to be heard and understood by the audience. In rock music, by contrast, the words of the songs are usually not as important as the beat, the rhythm, and the pure energy and emotion of the music. So how do you tell a complex story, like the one in *Rent*, through a musical score largely composed of rock?

Larson met the challenge head on by creating a hybrid of rock music and the sort of traditional music Broadway audiences are accustomed to. Of course, not everyone was pleased with the resulting score. Serious rock 'n' rollers thought Larson's music was not hardcore enough. But for the music to carry the story forward and still engage audiences, it had to be somewhat modified. In any case, the show was a huge hit. And it succeeded in bringing into musical theater a demographic that had largely ignored the genre—young people in their twenties and thirties who considered Broadway totally off limits.

Larson's *Rent* changed all that. Young people flocked to the show when it opened and through much of its twelve-year run. The word bohemia has a long history as a synonym for an artists' colony, a place characterized by residents who lead an unconventional life, rejecting the values and life choices of people who are more concerned with stability and financial security, and with being part of the status quo. Bohemians are more than willing to challenge social standards and live day by day, in the moment, instead of focusing on the future. And for many artists, the bohemian lifestyle is just the thing, at least when they're first starting out and burning with passion and the desire to create something new and revolutionary. The show's setting in the East Village, the city's "hip" neighborhood where cheap rents and a bohemian atmosphere attracted and continue to attract a large number of artists and other creative types, was important in establishing the mindset of the characters.

Bohemia in Fact and Fiction

Bohemia is not just a name for a city's artistic milieu. Bohemia is actually a region in the Czech Republic in Eastern Europe. At one time, Roma people (mistakenly referred to as Gypsies) were called *Bohemiens* in French. In the nineteenth century, poor artists living in the Latin Quarter of Paris were also known by this term. Henri Murger, a French writer, used the term to describe the artists in his series of stories set in the Latin Quarter in the 1840s and called it *Scenes de la Vie de Boheme* (*Scenes of the Bohemian Life*). The stories were drawn from Murger's own experience in the Latin Quarter as a young writer. Somewhat later, he turned his sketches into a play titled *La Vie de Bohème* (*The Bohemian Life*) and then into a novel. Both the play and the novel did well, and they firmly established in the public's mind the new meaning of bohemian.

In his introduction to *Scenes de la Vie de Boheme*, Murger notes that "Bohemia is a stage in artistic life. … Today, as of old, every man who enters on an artistic career, without any other means of livelihood than his art itself, will be forced to walk in the paths of Bohemia."

In that sense, the characters of Mark and Roger are true bohemians, and so are their friends. And the East Village where they live is the New York equivalent of the Latin Quarter in Paris, the setting of Henri Murger's book and play. But there's much more to the story than the similarity of settings between Larson's twentieth-century musical and Murger's nineteenth-century characterization of life in Bohemia.

La Bohème, Briefly

Enter Giacomo Puccini, composer of the nineteenth-century Italian opera *La Bohème*. The opera opens on Christmas Eve and unfolds in four acts, focusing on the lives and relationships of four impoverished bohemian characters: Rodolfo, a poet; Marcello, a painter; Schaunard, a musician; and Colline, a philosopher. The opera romanticizes their free-spirited lifestyle, glossing over the seamier side of life in the Latin Quarter of Paris.

One aspect of nineteenth-century life the opera doesn't gloss over is the prevalence of tuberculosis (TB), a life-threatening disease that reached epidemic proportions and was known as consumption at the time Puccini wrote the opera. The disease affected all classes of people but progressed more rapidly among the poor where malnutrition, overcrowding, and limited access to medical help typically meant a death sentence for anyone infected with TB.

The French writer Henri Murger based his 1851 novel *Scènes de la Vie de Bohème* on his own life.

The disease forms a dark backdrop to the lives of the characters in *La Bohème*, particularly Mimi, a poor seamstress dying from TB who has fallen in love with the poet Rodolfo. In the opera's fourth and final act, she begs to be taken back to the garret where she and Rodolfo first met. And there, with Rodolfo by her side, she slips into unconsciousness and dies.

Bringing the Past into the Present

Fast forward to the twentieth century—1989, to be exact. Playwright Billy Aronson envisions a new musical, a contemporary version of *La Bohème*. It seems like the perfect time to adapt the opera for a modern audience. Aronson sees many similarities between the bohemian Latin Quarter of Paris in the nineteenth century and the situation of young American artists near the turn of the century and the new millennium. All he needs is a composer to write the music. His connections led him to Jonathan Larson, who loved the idea of reinventing *La Bohème*.

Aronson and Larson began their collaboration. Their script was to follow the basic plot of Puccini's opera. But there were significant changes. For one thing, instead of the Latin Quarter, Larson wants the setting to be Manhattan's East Village. If any neighborhood could be called bohemian, it was certainly the East Village with its low rents, shabby storefronts, and hordes of young artists. Instead of TB running rampant through the lives of artists, causing sickness and premature death, the newest killer disease was AIDS, the acronym for acquired immunodeficiency syndrome.

Giacomo Puccini was an Italian composer. His 1895 opera, *La Bohème*, was iinspired by Henri Murger's novel.

AIDS is caused by a virus that attacks the body's immune system. The virus itself is called the human immunodeficiency virus, or HIV. If left untreated, it can progress to a full-blown case of AIDS, the final and most severe stage of HIV infection. The AIDS epidemic spread rapidly in the United States through the 1980s and into the 1990s, especially among the gay population. However, the virus was also being spread through drug injection with contaminated needles and heterosexual sex. In New York's East Village during the 1980s, a heroin epidemic on top of an AIDS epidemic claimed the lives of countless individuals. Documentarian David France recalls that in his East Village neighborhood, death "was inescapable. You would see people who were skinny, skinny skeletons trying to catch their breath, wheelchairs with men in their 20s, [with] lesions everywhere."

Larson wanted to call the show he and Aronson were working on *Rent*. But Aronson didn't like the title—until his partner pointed out that the word "rent" doesn't just mean the amount of money a tenant pays a landlord; it also means "torn," as in rent by grief. Several of Larson's friends had already died from AIDS. Heroin users sharing contaminated needles were easy prey for the disease. So were his sexual partners, one of whom may already have been infected with the virus.

In 1991, after two years of irregular collaboration, Larson succeeded in getting his partner's permission to continue the project on his own. And that's when it really took off. Larson, barely out of his twenties, was brimming over with ideas for the show. He wanted to infuse it with honest-to-goodness rock music and make Broadway stand up and take notice of a new kind of theater. *Rent* wouldn't shy away from controversial issues. Nor would it lean on the types of characters present in many Broadway shows. No way. The characters in *Rent* would reflect the

AIDS decimated communities like the East Village. This young man is one of countless AIDS sufferers.

people who lived hardscrabble lives in the East Village's bohemian community.

Rent—Child of *La Bohème* and So Much More

Let's focus on some of the major differences and similarities between Larson's creation and Puccini's *La Bohème*. We've already noted that both plays take place in a bohemian community, and in both settings, a raging disease is threatening the lives of the inhabitants: tuberculosis in the Latin Quarter of Paris; AIDS in the East Village of Manhattan. The main characters in both are struggling young artists and other nonconformists coping with poverty, searching for enduring love and a meaningful existence, and having to deal with heart-crushing loss and disappointment.

Larson didn't just update Puccini's masterful opera. Drawing upon a variety of sources, especially *La Bohème*, he created a high-energy fusion of musical styles—genuine, electrifying rock and the quieter storytelling music of Broadway theater in which the lyrics help carry the plot forward. They said it couldn't be done. But Larson proved his detractors wrong. Whatever its flaws and shortcomings, the rock opera *Rent* succeeded big time and won over the audience he most closely identified with—young, unconventional people like himself.

Composed of two acts, *Rent* doesn't pull any punches when it comes to revealing what the characters are facing in their lives and what their environment is like. In the first act, Collins, the philosopher character, is mugged on the street. The mugger steals his coat and leaves him beaten and bloodied. In the lot opposite the building where his friends Mark and Roger live, the homeless have put up a tent city. But if the owner of the property has his way, the tents will be pulled down and the people evicted.

Maureen, a performance artist, plans to stage her own one-person show in that very same lot as a way to protest the owner's callousness and greed. The owner's name is Benny. He used to share Mark and Roger's apartment with them, but after marrying into a wealthy family, he prefers comfort and security to bohemian poverty. He also happens to be Mark

PRINCIPAL CHARACTERS IN *LA BOHÈME*	PRINCIPAL CHARACTERS IN *RENT*
Rodolfo, a poet	Roger, an HIV-positive musician who is a recovering heroin addict.
Marcello, a painter	Mark, a filmmaker who wants to make a documentary about his friends.
Schaunard, a musician	Angel Dumott Schunard, a street musician and transvestite who has AIDS.
Colline, a philosopher	Tom Collins, a philosophy professor and political activist who also has AIDS. Angel and Collins become lovers.
Mimi, a frail, fragile seamstress dying from tuberculosis and in love with Rodolfo	Mimi Marquez, an exotic dancer who works at the Cat Scratch nightclub. Mimi is HIV-positive and in love with Roger.
Musetta, a singer	Maureen Johnson, a fiery performance artist with strong political views. She used to be Mark's girlfriend until she fell in love with Joanne.
Alcindoro, a respectable politician	Joanne Jefferson, a lesbian lawyer and Maureen's current girlfriend. Joanne's character is based on Alcindoro and another character, Marcello.
Benoit, a landlord	Benjamin "Benny" Coffin III, a landlord and former roommate of Mark and Roger.

and Roger's landlord and on Christmas Eve demands that they pay him what they owe him—a year's worth of back rent.

The principal characters in *Rent* are close cousins to the characters in Puccini's opera, but they're not identical. Their names are similar, but their personal identities reflect the times in which they are living.

In *Rent*, the first encounter between Mimi Marquez and Roger is nearly identical to the same scene in *La Bohème* when Mimi meets Rodolfo. In both scenes, Mimi asks Roger/Rodolfo to light her candle, which marks the start of their love affair. The lyrics of Larson's song "Light My Candle" are different from the words sung by Mimi and Rodolfo in the same scene, but the intent is the same—to show two young people discovering each other for the first time and falling in love.

In *La Bohème*, Mimi purposely leaves her room key behind as an excuse to return to Rodolfo's apartment. In *Rent*, Mimi Marquez also leaves a token behind—in this case, a small amount of heroin. With a lit candle, she'll not only be able to see in the darkness of her room but prepare a shot of heroin by heating it in a spoon. Puccini's Mimi, however, does not use drugs. As a hard-working seamstress, she needs candlelight in order to continue sewing at night.

By the third act in *La Bohème*, Rodolfo has abandoned Mimi. She thinks he left her out of jealousy, believing she was interested in someone else. At the end of the act, Rodolfo confides in his friend Marcello that he loves Mimi more than anything else in the world. The real reason he can't see her anymore is because Mimi is dying from

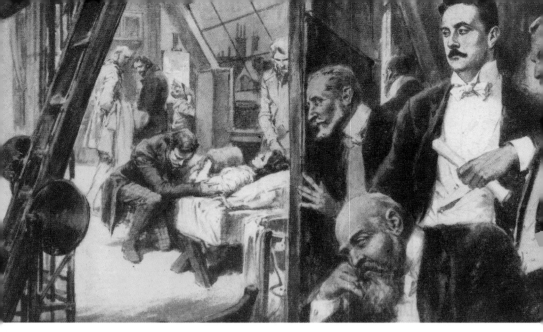
Pucccini and his collaborators watch the opening performance of *La Bohème* in Turin, Italy.

consumption, and he is simply too poor to take proper care of her. In *Rent*, the relationship between Mimi and Roger follows a similar trajectory. Roger is afraid of becoming involved with Mimi because she is a heroin addict and also because he knows, as an AIDS sufferer, he doesn't have long to live. He doesn't want Mimi to go through what he experienced after his former girlfriend April killed herself when she found out she was HIV-positive.

In Act II of *Rent*, the couple experiences a tumultuous relationship, breaking up and then reconciling more than once over the course of a year. Mimi's health continues to deteriorate, and her addiction to heroin shows no sign of diminishing. Roger temporarily leaves New York and heads to Santa Fe, New Mexico. But he can't get Mimi out of his mind. By Christmas Eve, one year later, he returns to New York ready to continue their relationship. Mimi, however, is nowhere to be found. She's been living on the streets in the dead of winter, and when Maureen and her lover Joanne bring Mimi into Roger and Mark's apartment, it's clear she's dying. She tells Roger how much she loves him, and Roger sings the song that she inspired. Then he confesses that he loves her in return.

At the end of *La Bohème*, Mimi dies from her illness. In despair, her lover Rodolfo embraces Mimi one last time. At the end of Larson's play, Mimi loses consciousness, and Roger believes she has died. But then, she opens her eyes, fully alive, and tells Roger and the others that she was near death when Angel (a principal character in the play who had recently died from AIDS) appeared in a white light and counseled her to go back and be with Roger.

Larson Mines His Own Life for Material

As fate would have it, *Rent* had its Off-Broadway preview performance in 1996, a century after the premiere performance of *La Bohème* in Italy. Puccini's opera, beginning on Christmas Eve in Paris, covers a span of several months in the lives of the characters. Larson's rock opera also begins on Christmas Eve. The action spans one complete year, ending on the following Christmas Eve. While *La Bohème* served as the main source of the plot, there were additional influences that went into making *Rent* a truly unique retelling of the story. One of these influences was Larson's own life. The industrial loft where the characters

Mark and Roger live was modeled after Larson's own apartment, where the bathtub was in the kitchen and a jerry-rigged stove was the only source of heat.

Larson ran an orange extension cord throughout his real-life apartment since there were so few outlets. In the stage version of his apartment, a similar cord is used. Because his actual buzzer didn't work, Larson had to throw his keys down to the street so visitors could let themselves into the building; in the play, Mark and Roger have to do the same. Like Roger and Maureen, Larson had a girlfriend who left him after falling for a woman. In *Rent*, Mark attends a meeting of Life Support, a support group for people with HIV. In his own life, Larson attended support meetings with a childhood friend who had been diagnosed HIV-positive. During the scene in which the meeting is taking place, the names of three of Larson's friends who died from AIDS are mentioned.

Some theater critics have insisted that *Rent* is much more than an updating of *La Bohème*. While the characters and the bohemian setting are similar, the rock opera is actually more of a creative response to Puccini's opera. *La Bohème* tells a tragic tale that ends with Mimi's death

Fact You May Not Know

RIVAL OPERAS

Puccini's rival composer Ruggero Leoncavallo also wrote an opera called *La Bohème*. It opened one year after Puccini's opera. Both operas ran simultaneously for about ten years until audiences decided their favorite was Puccini's. Its popularity has never waned.

In 2016, the London cast of *Rent* performed in a twentieth anniversary production of the show.

and her lover's sorrow; *Rent*, by contrast, is a celebration of life in which death, though present, does not destroy the characters' lifesaving capacity for joy and love. *Rent* is studded with references to life, like the Life Support group and the Life Café where the characters meet and sing "La Vie Bohème" ("The Bohemian Life"), in which they celebrate everything they love about life.

In the first act of *Rent*, the characters and their situation are clearly based on the first act of Puccini's opera. But once these are established, Larson pretty much goes his own way in creating characters whose problems and pursuits reflect the times in which they are living. The passion that fuels their lives and the play's faithfulness to real life are key to understanding why *Rent* had such a long and successful Broadway run and continues to be staged today.

Puccini's four-act opera *La Bohème* had its premiere performance in Turin, Italy on February 1, 1896. The opera was based more on the dramatized version of Henri Murger's book than on the book itself. Puccini composed the music, and his two collaborators Luigi Illica and Giuseppe Giacosa wrote the libretto, all of the spoken and sung words of the opera. Critics panned the opera; they argued that it was contrary to the tradition of Italian opera in which heroic characters experience profound emotions and passionate relationships. Critics also objected to the sort of life portrayed in *La Bohème.* The bohemian lifestyle, they said, was not appropriate for the stage. Poverty, disease, hunger—these facts of life, according to the critics, were better left out of serious opera.

Critics may have dismissed *La Bohème* as an unfortunate departure from Italian opera, but audiences loved it. To this day, it remains one of Puccini's most popular works, along with *Tosca* and *Madama Butterfly*. The four major characters in *La Bohème* are all young, destitute artists sharing an unheated garret in Paris's Latin Quarter in the 1830s. Rodolfo is a writer and poet. Marcello is a painter. Schaunard is a musician, and Colline is a philosopher. The opera begins on a bitter-cold Christmas Eve.

Shortly after his friends exit, leaving him alone in his attic apartment, Rodolfo hears someone knocking on the door. His unexpected visitor lives in the same building. Her name is Mimi, and she makes a poor living by embroidering fabrics with various kinds of flowers. Rodolfo can't help but notice how beautiful she is and is immediately

In *La Bohème,* Mimi dies from tuberculosis. Rodolfo, her lover, kneels at her bedside.

attracted to her, as she is attracted to him. She asks him to light her candle, the only source of light in her room. He can tell that Mimi is also very sick. Her face is pale, and soon after she enters, she faints from weakness. From this chance meeting, Rodolfo and Mimi fall in love. The story of their tragic relationship over four acts is the heart and soul of Puccini's opera.

One of the strongest reasons for the opera's enduring popularity is the composer's inclusion of ordinary, believable characters. For centuries, operas were dominated by extraordinary figures like kings and queens, gods and goddesses. Composers like Puccini understood that an increasing number of opera lovers preferred to see common folks on the stage experiencing the kinds of trials and tribulations that they experienced in their own lives. In *La Bohème* and other works by Puccini, the characters may be ordinary, and yet their lives are no less filled with passion and deep feelings. What they feel, we feel too, and when their hearts break, so do ours.

Chapter 2

From Page to Stage

The characters of Mark and Roger are aspiring artists living the bohemian life. For them, this means sacrificing comfort and security for the sake of one's art. Their neighborhood is multicultural and multiethnic, and their friends include junkies, an exotic dancer, a cross-dressing drummer, a professor of philosophy, and a performance artist. In the background of their lives lurks the ever-present threat of a mysterious disease—AIDS—that has reached epidemic proportions and devastated the gay community in particular.

> **We begin on Christmas Eve, with me, Mark, and my roommate, Roger. We live in an industrial loft on the corner of 11th Street and Avenue B, the top floor of what was once a music-publishing**

Opposite: In this London production of *Rent*, Ross Hunter and Billy Cullum appear as roommates Roger and Mark.

factory. Old rock-'n'-roll posters hang on the walls … We have an illegal wood-burning stove; its exhaust pipe crawls up to a skylight. All of our electrical appliances are plugged into one thick extension cord, which snakes its way out a window. Outside, a small tent-city has sprung up in the lot next to our building. Inside, we are freezing because we have no heat.

Jonathan Larson, the person credited as the composer and creator of *Rent*, didn't come up with the initial idea. That honor goes to a young playwright by the name of Billy Aronson. After graduating from Yale University with a degree in drama, Aronson moved to New York in 1983. In his free time, he often attended the Metropolitan Opera (the Met) at the Lincoln Center for the Performing Arts. That's where he first experienced *La Bohème* in all its heartbreaking glory.

Deeply affected by its universal themes of love and death, and its gripping musical score, Aronson envisioned a contemporary version of Puccini's opera, one that would use modern musical idioms to express the temper of the times. It was a great idea, but there was one big problem: Aronson couldn't compose music. So he went looking for someone who could. He turned to Ira Weitzman, the director of musical theater at Playwrights Horizons, an organization with which Aronson was connected, and Weitzman recommended two composers. One of them was Jonathan Larson.

Mark, a filmmaker, and Roger, a musician, share a rundown apartment in New York's East Village.

To get around town, Larson rode his bike or a barely serviceable car he named Rusty. For nine and a half years, he waited on tables at the Moondance Diner on Sixth Avenue in SoHo near New York's Greenwich Village. The job netted him just enough money to pay his living expenses while leaving him the time he needed to focus on writing music.

Larson may have been living the life of the struggling young artist, but none of his friends considered him poor. They

Before *Rent* became a hit, Jonathan Larson waited on tables in this New York diner.

remember him as someone with a wealth of good friends, a man who loved life and could always find something to celebrate in even the most common, everyday events.

In the spring of 1989, Billy Aronson met Larson for the first time. Larson had already enjoyed some success writing musicals, including a one-person show—*tick, tick...BOOM!*—about his own life and a question that constantly nagged him: Should he continue trying to make it as a composer, or should he give up and get a full-time job writing advertisement copy?

After getting in touch with him, Aronson headed over to Larson's apartment in the West Village. From the get-go, Larson loved the idea of updating *La Bohème*. His mind was already churning with ideas for how to accomplish this transformation. He told Aronson he wanted their show to be a rock musical that would appeal to the MTV generation

An early Larson musical, *tick, tick...BOOM!* explored the challenge of living as an artist.

and revolutionize musical theater, like *Hair* had done for an earlier generation.

Road Bumps Along the Way

One of the initial disagreements the collaborators experienced was over the tone and content of the lyrics. Larson composed the music for the lyrics that Aronson was writing. But he rejected Aronson's first attempts, which he thought sounded too much like songs from the early 1990s TV series *thirtysomething*. They agreed that the characters suffering from tuberculosis in Puccini's opera would have AIDS in *Rent*, and instead of a garret in nineteenth-century Paris, they would live in New York's bohemian East Village. The plot would pretty much follow the basic narrative in *La Bohème*, but the identities of the main characters and their relationships would need to be reimagined.

Their collaboration was anything but smooth sailing. As Aronson recalls, his partner could be very headstrong at times, insisting that a scene or song lyric go a certain way. No discussion. Collaboration for both men was a new experience, and both had problems expressing what was on their minds without sounding quarrelsome.

Once they had a working draft of the entire show, they recorded a demo cassette tape that would showcase the first three songs that Aronson had written. But then they hit another snag. Aronson wasn't sure about continuing with the project since he was worried about working for nothing if the show didn't go anywhere. Larson, on the other hand, was not ready to call it quits. Unable to come to an understanding, they decided to take a break from the project for an unspecified amount of time. While Aronson went to work on other plays, Larson turned his attention toward his performance piece, *tick, tick…BOOM!*

Going Solo

Two years later, he phoned Billy Aronson and told him he wanted to continue working on the show by himself. Larson offered to credit Aronson for coming up with the concept and to compensate him for his contributions if the show was ever produced.

Thankfully, Aronson accepted the terms of his former partner's proposal. The future of *Rent* was now entirely in

Larson's mother Nannette and *Hamilton* creator Lin-Manuel Miranda attend the 2014 opening performance of *tick, tick...BOOM!*

Jonathan Larson's capable hands. "It just got better and better," Aronson recalled. "He was clearly inspired." Part of Larson's inspiration and unflagging energy was the fact that *Rent* had become a vehicle for presenting his own life story. One other strong reason for Larson's decision to pursue the project on his own was the growing threat of AIDS and the toll it was taking on the community in which he lived. Larson wanted to make a difference, and putting the AIDS crisis in a play was one way to do just that. *Rent* would show AIDS sufferers as real people who deserved not only recognition but respect and love, as he had loved his friends who died from the disease.

By this time, Larson had radically transformed Billy Aronson's original script. In addition to incorporating details from his own life, Larson returned to the source of Puccini's opera, Henri Murger's nineteenth-century novel, *Scènes de la Vie Bohéme*. Instead of making the characters in *Rent* modern-day equivalents of the characters in *La Bohéme*, Larson went in a different direction: Collins and Angel (Colline and Schaunard in *La Bohéme*) are both gay. Maureen (Musetta) is bisexual, and Puccini's character Alcindoro has become Maureen's lesbian lover Joanne. The seamstress Mimi in *La Bohéme* dies at the end. In *Rent*, Mimi is an exotic dancer who has a near-death experience but then comes back to life.

The New York Theatre Workshop

In the summer of 1992, when Larson was riding his bike down East Fourth Street, he passed an old theater undergoing renovation. Larson's decision to park his bike and check out the theater marked the next leap forward in *Rent*'s journey to Broadway. It turned out that the New York Theatre Workshop (NYTW) had pulled out of its rental space in the West Village and moved to the East Village. The theater that Larson had stopped to investigate would be NYTW's new headquarters. Jim Nicola, the artistic director, was searching for a production that would introduce their new neighbors to NYTW and reflect the character of the East Village community.

Larson thought the theater was the perfect venue for his new musical. The next day, he went to the theater's business office and dropped off the script along with the demo tape. From director Jim Nicola's introduction to *Rent* that summer to a fully staged production four years later, in the winter of 1996, the script and the musical score went through multiple revisions. Along the way, the production team encountered a number of daunting obstacles that might have completely derailed the process and kept *Rent* from ever making it to Broadway.

Nicola was quick to pick up on the significance of Larson's work-in-progress. Not only would it reflect NYTW's new location, it would also be the first musical NYTW had ever produced. Nicola also sensed that *Rent* was just the thing to revitalize Broadway shows: "I thought that this composer had the potential to write music which would fulfill the integrity of the pop song and the integrity of the theater song."

Going Deeper

But there were problems. One of them had to do with the very nature of the script. The music was terrific. But the songs lacked a spine—a strong story line that could hold the songs together and give audiences the experience that comes from a convincing narrative. Nicola felt the show was too much like a concert instead of a coherent story that would connect emotionally with people. Another problem, besides Larson's weakness as a storyteller, was a certain amount of "political incorrectness" in the show. For example, he

Michael Greif, the original director of *Rent*, appears here with Daphne Rubin-Vega from the original cast.

wanted to include an ensemble cast that would play the roles of homeless people living in tents on a vacant lot. But Nicola felt it was wrong to "put actors onstage and use them as a chorus of cute homeless people. It's demeaning, it's [offensive]." In early versions of the play, the homeless characters are portrayed as a nondescript group without individual identities.

Similarly, some of the characters, particularly the lesbian characters, seemed more like cardboard props. Larson's close friend Lisa Hubbard "talked to him a lot about the lesbian characters. I felt at first that he didn't know how pat [stereotypical] they were. They didn't feel like they were real people." As a gay woman, Hubbard wanted Larson to go more deeply into their characters and not shrink from showing them relating and behaving like actual lesbian lovers.

Michael Greif, who directed the NYTW production, pushed Larson to humanize the artist characters, mainly the two roommates Mark and Roger. According to Greif, Larson needed to "depict them as people who could also make mistakes, could be self-deluded, who were not right all the time." Larson, in Greif's view, had a tendency to present the artists in his play as superior and self-loving in ways that might turn off audiences.

The Producers Have Cold Feet

Jim Nicola continued to have reservations about producing *Rent*, despite how much he liked working with Larson. To convince Nicola to take a chance on his show, Larson organized a staged reading at NYTW in order to attract potential investors. The reading took place on June 17, 1993. A lot of people in the funding community, especially Off-Broadway producers, attended the reading. While the music was a big hit, the play as a whole failed to impress them. Jeffrey Seller, one of the producers, brought three of his friends to the reading. Two of them left during intermission. "The third said that [the show] couldn't be saved and that Jonathan should get on with his life." Seller recalled other comments like "Well, he's promising, a good songwriter, but [the show] is a big chaotic mess."

The show desperately needed financial backing. Larson took his project to other theaters. Some of them started

Mimi and Roger perform in *Rent*'s twentieth anniversary production.

working on *Rent* but then stopped because of how difficult Larson could be. Then, in 1994, he received a $45,000 Richard Rodgers Development Grant—enough money to finance a NYTW production of *Rent*. Larson and Jim Nicola agreed that Michael Greif, a rising star in the directing community, would be just the person to direct *Rent*. A workshop performance was scheduled for the fall of 1994. But before that could happen, Larson's script needed more work. The characterizations were weak, and the plot was confusing. But everyone was on the same page when it came to the music: it was fantastic! No doubt about it.

Both Nicola and Greif felt that Larson stuck too closely to *La Bohème* and to his own experience as a struggling artist. In order for the show to grow wings of its own and really take off, Larson would need to get clear about what he wanted to say and say it in a more concise way, partly by clarifying the subplots, which were confusing and interfered with the main storyline. Larson was tasked with keeping the focus on the storytelling now that the music and the basic structure of the show were in place. Nicola encouraged him to understand "who are these [characters], what do they want?"

Sweet Smell of Success

To help Larson stay on course as he worked on the latest draft, Nicola recommended that he come up with one sentence that would encompass the whole story, from start to finish. In September

David Merino, as Angel, sings "Today 4 U."

1994, the NYTW began putting together a cast for the first workshop production. The casting team hired people with an exciting range of backgrounds, including those with substantial acting experience as well as people who were primarily singers or worked in some other creative field like performance art. They even went to a gay bar across the street from the theater "to see if anyone knew any drag queens who wanted to be in a play," according to Martha Banta, an assistant director at NYTW. Director Michael

Greif "was looking for compelling, rough, intelligent actor-singers. I thought that we really needed some sort of kooky, authentic folks to pull it off, to teach me and Jonathan [Larson] things."

Tim Weil was hired to serve as the show's musical director. It was a natural choice; he had been the pianist for the auditions. With Weil on board, the music underwent a major transformation. Larson and his recording engineer Steve Skinner had originally wanted to rely primarily on synthesizers. Larson even imagined having the music performed exclusively by computers. But Weil opted to use a real rock 'n' roll band to complement the scruffy world of the show. In his notes for the workshop script, Larson made it clear that he wanted the sound mix to blend the music of Broadway with the sound of a rock concert. The drums and the electric guitars should be loud and clear, he wrote, but without overpowering the lyrics, which needed to be heard and understood like traditional Broadway show tunes.

Rehearsals ran for two weeks followed by ten workshop performances, from October 29 to November 6, 1994. Audiences were wild about the show, and by the last weekend, it was sold out. Best of all, three important producers came to see *Rent*, and all three were greatly impressed. In fact, they loved the show so much, they decided "then and there to do the deal," according to Allan Gordon, one of the producers. But they wanted the creative team (Larson, Greif, and Nicola) to continue developing the show. According to Jeffrey Seller, *Rent* was a "brilliant collage" that needed focusing.

The producers put up $200,000 to keep Larson's show alive and ready to go forward into the next stage of development. But then Greif relocated to San Diego to direct another show. Beginning in January 1995, he was temporarily unavailable to collaborate with Larson, who was expected to give the show a tighter structure.

Up in the Air

Larson was supposed to turn in a completed rewrite of the script by September. That would provide enough time for cast and crew to have the show ready by December for a series of preview performances. But the show had to be postponed until January 1996, since Greif was still in San Diego and Larson had not met his September deadline. He didn't finish the rewrite until late October, at which time a reading was scheduled. In its latest incarnation, the show opened with the funeral of one of the central characters. Everything that followed, in this new version, was a flashback.

In addition, Larson had complicated the plotlines of other characters and written new songs, some of which were not well received. To make matters worse, the producers were getting nervous. A lot of money was on the line and given all the problems in the script, they feared they might have no choice but to "pull the plug" on the whole project. Also, NYTW was looking at a tight budget for the coming year. They couldn't afford to launch a project that appeared headed for failure.

No one wanted to tell Larson just how "up in the air" things were. They knew how invested he was in the show and how important it was for him to see *Rent* produced by a reputable theater company. He was already thirty-five and had been living in New York for thirteen years without having had one of his shows produced. Canceling *Rent* would crush him. "If this show doesn't open, I'm going to explode," he told Jeffrey Seller, one of the producers.

Getting Down to Business

Larson swallowed his pride and buckled down to rewriting the show in line with his producers' concerns. The opening funeral scene was scrapped, so the action of the play would no longer be a flashback. Anthony Rapp, an original cast member, commented positively about the latest rewrites: "[They] were so much better, and to see that transformation—it seemed like something had cracked open. … [The script] took this giant leap. It felt to me like Jonathan had to dig deeper into himself. Rather than painting the picture, he had to become part of it."

Auditions began in late August for the staged production scheduled to open in January. The casting process was extremely arduous, since the roles demanded superior singing ability along with decent acting chops. In the course of the auditions, the actors who were chosen were more racially and ethnically diverse than the performers for the first NYTW reading. After four months of auditioning almost a thousand people, fifteen people were finally selected as the definitive cast of *Rent*. In December, Larson presented the revised script along with his one-sentence distillation of the entire show: "*Rent* is about a community celebrating life, in the face of death and AIDS, at the turn of the century."

Earlier that year, in October, Larson had quit his job at the Moondance Diner. He was banking on *Rent* becoming a successful show and on receiving enough to live on from NYTW during the rehearsal period. But the checks weren't forthcoming, and by November, Larson was flat broke. One night in early January, he and his friend Lisa Hubbard planned on going to the movies. Unable to afford the price of a ticket, he had to sell some of his books and borrow five dollars from Lisa.

On January 2, 1996, the cast performed the first read-through of the recently revised script. Their audience was the show's producers and the staff of NYTW. When it was over, Jeffrey Seller "was just in heaven. I went up to Jonathan and said, 'You done good.'"

Something's Wrong

Technical rehearsals began on January 21. Larson's dream was finally coming true. He had begun working on *Rent* seven years earlier, and now it was only a matter of days before the general public would have their first exposure to what would become a legend in the history of musical theater. On the evening of the first tech rehearsal, Larson went out for dinner and then returned to the rehearsal space. While sitting next to the director during the second act, he got up and walked toward the back of the house. Out of the blue, he felt a sharp pain in his chest and staggered to the lobby. From there, he cried out, "You better call 911; I think I'm having a heart attack." Larson went back into the theater and lay down on the floor.

Over the next few days, Larson was rushed to the emergency room of two different hospitals after experiencing severe chest pains. Doctors at Cabrini Hospital concluded he was suffering from food poisoning and pumped out his stomach. At St. Vincent's, the diagnosis was a bad case of the flu. In both cases, Jonathan was sent home to rest.

The final dress rehearsal was scheduled for January 24. Despite how awful Larson felt, he forced himself to get up and leave the apartment, even having his hair cut before arriving at the theater. The cast performed *Rent* before a full house. At the end of the show, the audience gave them a standing ovation. There was no doubt about it. The show was a hit, and Larson couldn't have been prouder or happier. Hearing that applause and knowing how much the audience had loved the performance—"that was the crowning moment of his creative life," ensemble member Timothy Britten Parker recalled.

Later that evening, Anthony Tommasini, a theater critic from the *New York Times*, interviewed Larson about the show and his personal history. It was the first and last interview he ever gave. Larson was supposed to join directors Greif and Nicola for a late-night huddle to critique the dress rehearsal. But because the interview had lasted an hour, they agreed to meet the next morning over breakfast. Larson left the theater and went home in a cab.

The Hardest Time for All

The next morning, the creative team and the cast members got shocking news: Jonathan had died. His roommate, Brian Carmody, had come home around 3:30 a.m. and found him on the kitchen floor. It was later revealed that an aneurysm in his aortic artery had ruptured. The chest pain he had experienced earlier in the week was the first indication that something was terribly wrong. Eventually, the two hospitals that had treated him were charged with misdiagnosis and mistreatment. His condition was congenital. If detected in time, an aortic aneurysm can be surgically repaired, with an 80 to 90 percent rate of full recovery.

The reaction of Jeffrey Seller was probably typical of how people were responding to the news: "I was in shock. I remember falling against the wall with fear and surprise and not understanding how this could be. ... Someone you know and had affection and love for has gone somewhere, and you don't know where it is. I cried all day."

Larson's death was the biggest and most daunting obstacle confronted by the cast and production crew. He had died on the very same day that *Rent* was supposed to open in a series of preview performances. Should the previews be canceled and the show postponed to a much later date? At NYTW, it was decided that the best way to honor Larson's life and the vision that inspired him to create *Rent* was to go forward. Greif believed that Jonathan "would want his work to be heard." That night's opening preview was cancelled. Instead, the cast would remain seated and perform a sing-through of the show for friends and family only—without any costumes or lighting changes. Jonathan's parents Al and Nan, hearing about their son's death, had flown to New York from their home in New Mexico.

Things went according to plan until the final scene of the first act, when the cast members were singing "La Vie Bohème" in what is supposed to be a neighborhood café. The energy of the lyrics and the intense emotions everyone was feeling needed an outlet. Unable to restrain themselves any longer, the actors spontaneously rose from their seats and danced their way through the song while standing on tables—performing this number just the way it had been originally blocked. For the second act, the tables were removed from the stage, and the cast pulled out all the stops, performing entirely on their feet.

Preview performances provide an opportunity to see how audiences are responding to the material and to make additional changes before opening night when the press is invited. In the case of *Rent*, Jonathan's absence meant that the creative team would have to second-guess what he would have wanted. They had two and a half weeks to make the necessary changes without sacrificing the integrity of Jonathan's vision. Fortunately, Greif and the others had access to Jonathan's notes as well as the experience of working with him. So their choices were made with great care to make the show as consistent as possible with how Jonathan would have wanted to proceed.

And they succeeded. The show opened on February 13, 1996 and received glowing reviews. The one that really got the ball rolling was by Ben Brantley of the *New York Times*.

Word-of-mouth and Brantley's review started a stampede of people wanting to see *Rent*. Tickets were flying out the door. The day after opening night, the first month of performances was completely sold out. Given its popularity, the show was extended for an additional month.

What's Next?

Clearly, *Rent* had outgrown NYTW. The show needed a much bigger space in order to accommodate the rapidly growing audience. The company was faced with another dilemma: Should the show remain downtown where it had been born and nurtured, or should it move uptown to the big time—Broadway? And if it went to Broadway, would they be selling out to commercialism and the lure of big bucks? Of course, they could always take the show to an Off-Broadway venue and see how well it did. Coming to a decision was no easy matter. Some people thought Broadway audiences would object to the content of the show. Adam Pascal, one of the actors in *Rent*, feared that the show would lose "artistic credibility and content" if it were produced on Broadway.

After much discussion and argument, the company decided to go for broke and move the show to Broadway. Now the search began for an appropriate theater. Not an easy job. Finally, the company decided on the Nederlander. According to Jeffrey Seller, "It was the right theater in the right place." One of its most attractive features was its dilapidated condition—a perfect environment in which to present a show about the rough side of East Village life.

Rent won the Pulitzer Prize for drama in 1996. Sadly, Jonathan Larson had died a few months earlier.

A Dream Come True

On April 2, the media announced that Jonathan Larson had been awarded the Pulitzer Prize for drama for *Rent*. On April 29, *Rent* opened on Broadway. The audience for the premiere performance at the Nederlander Theater included celebrities like George Clooney, Michelle Pfeiffer, and Barbara Walters. TV crews mobbed the theater. The opening was like a Hollywood spectacular. For members of the company, the event was a bittersweet experience, exhilarating and sad at the same time. The words of the show's choreographer Marlies Yearby sum up the experience: "The journey to Broadway was such an intense road. ... Everybody was still grieving [for Jonathan], but

Fact You May Not Know

ROCK-A-BYE BABY

Jonathan Larson's sister Julie lived on the West Coast. Late at night, after Jonathan finished writing a song, he would sometimes phone Julie. "Listen," he'd say, and then play the song for her. His songs became lullabies for Julie's children.

you also wanted to jump for joy, because it was an opening for people. We had such a rough ride; by opening night, we were *Rent*ed."

Don Summa, a press agent, described the first few minutes of the show's opening: "When the show started, Adam [who played Roger] walked on, the cast walked on and everybody in the audience just stood up. Then everybody sat down, and Anthony [who played Roger's roommate Mark] said, 'We dedicate this and every performance to the memory of Jonathan Larson,' and then everybody just stood up again, cheering and applauding and screaming and whooping."

DRAMATURG TO THE RESCUE

Nicola greatly respected Jonathan Larson as an innovative composer but feared that his ability to tell a straightforward story was not equal to his musical gifts. So he hired a New York University professor to work with Larson as a dramaturg, someone who helps refine and clarify an artist's vision.

Enter Lynn Thomson. As someone with a great deal of theater experience, she proved to be an invaluable collaborator. Working closely with Larson, she encouraged him to go more deeply into his characters and to learn the art of storytelling as a way to bring his vision into focus. She taught him to see how a well-told story has a very definite structure, and for Larson, a musician more than a playwright, this was an exciting new field to explore. Thomson thought Larson had so far written a cartoon. Her job, as she saw it, was to help him turn it into a drama. According to Janet Charleston, Larson's longtime girlfriend, his writing had seemed "more surface, like he didn't get down as far as he needed to. He would present these major profound subjects, but they didn't go deep enough."

To reach that deeper place, Thomson had Larson rewrite the biographies he had created for the characters. She wanted him to provide more detail about their lives. This and other exercises succeeded in bringing deeper emotional life and greater authenticity to his characters. Larson also moved beyond *Rent*'s one-sided depiction of people with AIDS. He wanted to believe that it was possible to know you are dying and yet be capable of living "in the moment" without feeling overwhelmed by anger or despair. But thanks in part to some intense discussions with Michael Greif, the show's director, Larson was willing to change how his characters were handling their disease. Instead of only showing them coming to terms and living at peace with AIDS, he allowed them to express their anger and rage at key points within the show.

Larson owed a debt of gratitude to Lynn Thomson. Her expertise and her understanding of the importance of a tightly structured narrative helped make *Rent* a major Broadway success. But for Thomson, gratitude wasn't enough compensation for all her hard work and the contributions she made to the show. In November 1996, she filed a lawsuit against the Larson estate in Manhattan Federal Court, claiming she was a coauthor of the play and therefore entitled to royalties (a percentage of the profits). However, the judge in the case ruled otherwise. He concluded that Thomson had contributed some material that could be copyrighted but was not entitled to royalties. Two years later, in 1998, an out-of-court settlement was reached that satisfied both parties.

Chapter 3

Broadway by Storm

I n these dangerous times, when it seems that the world
is ripping apart at the seams, we can all learn how to
survive from those who stare death squarely in the face
every day and [we] should reach out to each other and bond
as a community, rather than hide from the terrors of life at
the end of the millennium.

—Jonathan Larson, in a statement he wrote shortly
before his death and left on his computer.

Rent's premiere in 1996 coincided with the premiere of
Puccini's opera *La Bohème* one hundred years earlier, in
Turin, Italy. Audiences loved *Rent* from opening night to the
day it officially ended its Broadway run twelve years later, on
September 7, 2008, after 5,123 performances and numerous
awards, including Tony Awards for Best Musical, Best Book,

Opposite: Rent was performed in Broadway's Nederlander Theatre from
1996 to 2008.

Jonathan Larson's sister Julie holds up two of the awards her brother received posthumously for *Rent*.

Best Original Score, and Best Featured Actor. The popularity of the show was so great that people lined up outside the theater hours before the performance began. Soon after *Rent* arrived on Broadway, the producers decided to offer discounted tickets for the first two rows of seats. People who couldn't afford the standard price for most Broadway shows would now be able to see *Rent* for only twenty dollars. Many of these people came from the same demographic the show was targeting—young people between the ages of fifteen and thirty-five who might otherwise have never been interested in musical theater. The show was about them—their hopes and fears, their struggle to forge a life based on their ideals and values, even if this meant living in a shoddy apartment and earning just enough to survive.

Selling a limited number of cheap tickets also served another, less altruistic purpose: The long lines outside the theater helped market the show by demonstrating how immensely popular it was. It was such a successful marketing strategy that other Broadway theaters began copying what the Nederlander was doing with *Rent*.

The cheap tickets went on sale two hours before the next show began. During the week, the line began to form around noon. On weekends, it typically began twenty-four hours in advance. Hardcore fans were willing to camp out on the sidewalk overnight in order to be sure of getting a ticket. These fans became known as "Rentheads" or "Squatters." In the cold weather, some came prepared with their own survival kits, consisting of blankets or sleeping bags, pup tents, food, reading material, and plastic tarps in case of rain. The really devoted fans of *Rent* came back more than once for a front-row seat. A medical student from New Jersey saw the show more than a dozen times. Another young man waited in line more than three dozen times! That's serious brand loyalty.

One devoted *Rent* fan who frequently waited in line to buy a $20 ticket found watching the show a "cathartic experience" that took her "from joy to excitement to sorrow and back again in just over two hours." No matter how many times she'd been part of the audience, she was still "profoundly affected" by "the tremendous talent and energy of the cast [and] the music."

When she was thirteen years old, Kathryn Utke saw the movie version of *Rent* for the first time at her school's movie night in St. Paul, Minnesota. The experience changed her life. She had never before seen gay couples on the screen or watched a movie with so many racially diverse characters. And the music, for Kathryn, was overpowering. During a trip to her grandparents' house, she talked her parents into stopping at a Barnes & Noble store so she could buy the CD and upload it into her computer. The movie moved her to tears and inspired her "lifelong obsession with musicals":

> Jonathan Larson made a piece of work about himself, his friends, and the life that they lead, telling their stories through the music that he loved, and in turn, allowed future artists to do the same on a wider scale.

During the heyday of the show's popularity, the people willing to wait for hours to buy a ticket were typically in their teens and twenties. They were likely to watch music videos on MTV and listen to bands like Green Day. Until *Rent* made its appearance, attending a Broadway show was not on their radar. Not only were these shows too expensive, they had very little connection with what the younger generation was going through in a time when the AIDS crisis was peaking and drug addiction was becoming more

Billboards announce the latest Broadway shows in New York's Times Square.

prevalent. *Rent* offered the kind of raw truthfulness most musicals avoided. According to Utke, young people with limited means could now afford to "see themselves reflected on stage for the first time."

Professional theater critics who attended a performance of *Rent*, with few exceptions, came away from the theater with stars in their eyes. *Variety*'s reviewer, Jeremy Gerard, had this to say about the show on April 29, the day after the opening:

> The final musical entry in the 1995–96 season, *Rent* is the best show in years, if not decades.

Larson, on the cusp of 36 when he died of an aortic aneurysm, wrote songs in a wide range of pop idioms, from rock anthems and ballads to gospel to loping Western laments to old-fashioned Broadway showstoppers. ... In a season full of surprises, *Rent* is the pinnacle. ... [and] proves Broadway's enduring attraction for the most important new work the theater is producing. ... It's going to earn a lot of money, because everyone will want to savor its pleasures. *Rent* makes the musical theater joyously important again.

One of the many enthusiastic reviews that pushed the show into the public's eye and made it one of the hottest tickets in town was written by Ben Brantley, chief theater critic for the *New York Times*:

This vigorous tale of a marginal band of artists in Manhattan's East Village, a contemporary answer to *La Bohème*, rushes forward on an electric current of emotion that is anything but morbid. Sparked by a young, intensely vibrant cast ... and sustained by a glittering, inventive score, the work finds a transfixing brightness in characters living in the shadow of AIDS. Puccini's ravishingly melancholy work seemed, like many operas of its time, to romance death; Mr. Larson's spirited score and lyrics defy it.

The Majestic and the St. James are Broadway theaters located on 44th Street in midtown Manhattan.

Not everyone was bowled over by the show. David Rakoff, a Canadian-born American writer, saw the musical in his twenties. He wasn't too impressed:

> In *Rent*, the characters live out their seasons of love in huge lofts. Some of them have AIDS, which is coincidentally also the name of a dreaded global pandemic that is still raging and has killed millions of people worldwide. In *Rent*, however, AIDS seems to be a disease that renders one cuter and cuter.

Then there's Frank Rich, a highly respected columnist and essayist. His reviews have been known to make or break a new Broadway show, so getting his endorsement meant a real boost in ticket sales. Rich saw a NYTW performance of *Rent* before it moved to Broadway. In a *New York Times* op-ed published on March 2, 1996, he had this to say about the show:

> Two weeks ago, at a 150-seat theater in the East Village, a rock opera called *Rent* ... came out of nowhere to earn the most ecstatic raves of any American musical in the two decades since *A Chorus Line*. And now the world is rushing to catch up. ...
>
> *Rent* is all the critics say it is. ...
>
> The night I saw *Rent* at the New York Theatre Workshop. ... People were riveted, as I was, by the raw exuberance of characters who keep

Original cast members Wilson Jermaine Heredia (Angel) and Adam Pascal (Roger) were nominated for Tony awards.

fighting and creating and reaching out no matter how strong their fears—whether of death in a plague or of marginalization in the ruthless new post-industrial economy that frightens many Americans on the lower rungs.

The Emotional Impact on the Cast

For cast members, the experience of performing in *Rent* strongly affected their own lives. One of the prevailing themes in the show is the importance of connection, of feeling that you're part of a community in which your life matters and where you can expect to receive support and validation for the person you are. In his one-sentence summary of the show, Jonathan Larson said, "*Rent* was about a community." And the community featured in the show is a closely connected group of young artists and political activists sharing similar interests, beliefs, and ways of being in the world. The life revealed in *Rent* is the life an entire generation was living, a life that had never before been depicted in Broadway musicals.

But *Rent*'s appeal reaches beyond the fifteen to thirty-five age range. In the course of its twelve-year run, the show evolved into a multigenerational attraction. Jonathan's dad Al Larson noted, "*Rent* hits home with people of all ages. I see people with gray hair in the audience and I think, 'What are they doing?' That's one of my regrets, that I can't tell [my son] how good a job he did, how enduring his message is."

When Larson was alive, he loved to organize an annual holiday potluck supper—the Peasant Feast. He began this tradition in 1985 with a former roommate, Ann Egan. They would invite close friends, people who lived in the neighborhood, even people they may have just met on the street. As his dad pointed out, "Jonathan surrounded himself with terrific people, caring people. The Peasant Feast: that's part of his legacy." He wanted to bring the sense of community that infused this holiday ritual to the cast of *Rent*. To that end, he invited all the actors to the Peasant Feast. During rehearsals, "everyone worked hard to cultivate a family atmosphere similar to the kind of community feeling people experienced at the Peasant Feast." Rehearsals began with the entire cast singing "Seasons of Love," a popular song from *Rent* about measuring your life in love.

The original *Rent* cast celebrates the tenth anniversary of the show in 2006.

The life portrayed in *Rent* is a life lived in community where the love comes through loud and strong. And the strength of that love extended to the actors' offstage life. "The energy we bring to it, the connection we have offstage, transfers. People ask us if we love each other as much as it looks like we do, and we do," said Adam Pascal, a member of the original cast. Fredi Walker, who played Joanne, a lesbian lawyer, in the original cast, feels "Jonathan's spirit is part of what made this piece what it is. You get what you put out, and he put out so very much. *Rent* works because it hits things that everybody understands."

Jonathan Larson hoped that audiences with little or no connection with people living on the fringes of society

Mimi and Roger in a scene from Rent's 20th Anniversary Tour in 2016.

would leave with a bit more empathy and compassion, instead of prejudice, fear, or even hatred. Timothy Britten Parker, a member of the ensemble, attributes much of the success of *Rent* to its compassion for those whom mainstream society has tended to ignore, stigmatize, or stereotype: people who are "sick, poor, or gay or live what some might call an alternative lifestyle."

Parker also feels that *Rent* "reminds people … for the first time that these are lives of quality, that they have as much value as any other life. It's such a powerful message, and that was part of Jonathan's life."

Rent: A Rock Opera?

The producers of *Rent* were very involved in its marketing and how it was presented to the public. Jeffrey Seller noted, "An innovative show demands an innovative [marketing] campaign." One aspect of the campaign was to avoid labeling the show. None of the ads said, "*Rent*, the Broadway musical." Kevin McCollum, another producer,

Broadway Run:
Apr. 29, 1996–Sept. 7, 2008

Broadway Box Office Gross: $274.2 million

Number of Broadway Performances: 5,123

Awards Won:
Tony Awards for Best Musical
Best Book
Best Original Score
Best Featured Actor (Wilson Jermaine Heredia)
Pulitzer Prize for Drama
plus 12 other awards

Source: TheWrap.com, IMDB.com

agreed with his colleague: "We don't call it a musical or an opera, because it is what you bring to it. It's written in a very traditional musical theater style, in terms of its structure, like *Gypsy* or *Fiddler on the Roof*, Jonathan's favorite musicals."

Still, *Rent* was designed to appeal to a young, hip, urban audience. The energy and immediacy they were seeking mainly came from the rock concerts they attended— not from more conservative Broadway shows. Larson had wanted to change that. McCollum remarks that Larson's friends and other young people "weren't exposed to musical storytelling. *Rent* is musical storytelling, which is why we did not market it as a '90s rock opera."

In 1996, when *Rent* made its Broadway debut, it was competing with popular, long-running musicals like *Phantom of the Opera, Les Misérables, Beauty and the Beast*, and *Cats*. These shows were elaborately staged productions, with fabulous costumes, lush musical scores, and all the other trappings of traditional Broadway blockbusters. When *Rent* came along, one of the first things audience members might have noticed was the condition of the Nederlander Theatre. The producers wanted to re-create the downtown feel of the New York Theatre Workshop. They also wanted to evoke the atmosphere of bohemian life that is such an integral part of the show. The brick wall of the Nederlander was used as the back wall of the set. In traditional Broadway productions, anything that is the least bit unattractive is usually hidden or masked. But this was not the case with *Rent*. The whole stage was used to represent the downscale apartment where Roger and Mark

The Broadway cast of *Les Misérables*, a musical based on a nineteenth-century French novel

THE MARKETING CAMPAIGN FOR *RENT*

When *Rent* moved uptown to Broadway, the producers hired Drew Hodges, the founder and CEO of Spot Design, to create an ad campaign that would match the edginess and roughness of the show. Hodges was just the guy to accomplish this. He was pretty edgy himself. When a former landlord wouldn't allow him to keep a dog in his apartment, he decided to give his dog's name to his own theatrical ad agency, Spot Design.

He and his team didn't believe in anchoring their work in an identifiable style. Their approach was to treat each show as a one-of-a-kind event. The advertising "has to be true to the experience of that show...every show's voice begins with 'I want you to think of this show this way.'" At the time of *Rent*'s Broadway debut, people were skeptical that theatergoers would pay seventy-five dollars to watch a bunch of kids in their twenties sing about the bohemian life. Hodges figured that if *Rent* were "imaged correctly," it would attract people in the twenty-five to forty-five age range—the very demographic that tended to stay away from Broadway shows.

Hodges's pitch to Jeffrey Seller and Kevin McCollum, the producers of *Rent*, worked like a charm. They hired him to "write the copy, make the newspaper ads, then the TV commercial." Hodges in turn hired Amy Quip, an innovative and cutting-edge photographer, to design a poster for *Rent*.

The producers asked themselves what would happen if Roger and Mark, the roommate artists in the show, had to create all the marketing materials? What would the results look like? That's where Amy came in. She took photos of the cast members and created a montage that became one of *Rent*'s first ads. The montage also served as the artwork on the front cover of the cast recording. In order to attract the intended audiences and project the desired image, Hodges opted to focus on the characters and to convey the warmth and emotional vitality they project on stage. The producers had begun thinking about the show's logo in 1995, when it was still in development. They loved Hodges's concept for the logo because it looked like the show's artist characters could have designed it. The model for the logo was made with stencil and black masking tape and resembled the POST NO BILLS signs that could be seen at construction sites around New York.

live. (The same space was also used for other settings in the show without any elaborate set changes.) Moreover, there's no curtain across the front of the stage, and the backdrops aren't continuous, so the audience is able to see what's going on behind the scenes.

Instead of a full-piece orchestra performing the score, *Rent* used a five-member rock band. The players were onstage and visible to the audience through the entire show. One of the challenges the musicians faced was how to deliver authentic-sounding rock music in ways that didn't drown out the lyrics, which carried the narrative forward and therefore needed to be audible. Jonathan Larson wanted to merge rock music with theater music—not an easy task since these very different genres would normally clash. Jeff Potter, the drummer in the band, attributed the success of the music to Tim Weil, the musical director of *Rent*: "[He] knew how to make the music serve the drama but maintain the energy of pop. The [score] isn't so subservient to the drama that it loses the passion."

The producers chose not to label the show a rock opera, but because the show is sung (with only a few lines

SOMETHING BORROWED
Roger, the musician in *Rent*, strums his guitar at various times during the show. The melody he plays is an aria from Puccini's opera *La Bohème* called "Musetta's Waltz."

of spoken dialogue), it is technically an opera in which Larson deployed a number of classic musical techniques, like "quodlibet," in which different melodies are playing at the same time. Each has its own rhythm, but together they work in harmony. To hear what this sounds like, listen to a performance of the song "Light My Candle" from *Rent*.

Anthony Tommasini, the *Times* critic who interviewed Larson shortly before his death, advised composers to respect the differences between opera and musicals. He felt that Larson did just that:

> Here was a work specifically inspired by Puccini's [*La*] *Bohème*, also a tale of young artists struggling with love affairs, poverty and disease. But Larson thought the best way to pay homage to *Bohème* was not to mimic opera but to write an up-to-date, pop-infused, sophisticated musical-theater score. Yes, Larson was attempting to bring rock and pop styles into the musical-theater heritage. But *Rent* is a words-driven musical in the honored tradition.

"SEASONS OF LOVE"

Jonathan Larson wrote all of the music for *Rent*. Most of the songs are memorable, but the one that stands out as a real showstopper is "Seasons of Love." The entire cast performs the song at the top of Act II as they stand in a line along the edge of the stage. In 2005, when the movie version of *Rent* was released, "Seasons of Love" took the #68 spot on Billboard's "Hot 100" singles. On Apple's iTunes, it reached the #2 spot in the soundtrack category.

The original cast recording of the music from *Rent* was made in 1996. The album included a new arrangement of "Seasons of Love" performed by Stevie Wonder. Of all the songs from *Rent*, "Seasons of Love" was the one that got the most airplay on radio. Like the song "Aquarius" from the musical *Hair*, it was one of the few show tunes to become a mainstream hit. The original *Rent* cast also performed "Seasons of Love" at the Democratic National Convention in 1996.

For many young people in their twenties and thirties, the song was a powerful expression of how they saw the world and their place in it. Here are the opening verses:

> 525,600 minutes
>
> 525,000 moments so dear
>
> 525,600 minutes
>
> How do you measure, measure a year?

In daylights, in sunsets, in midnights, in cups of coffee

In inches, in miles, in laughter, in strife

In 525,600 minutes

How do you measure a year in the life?

That question, "How do you measure a year in the life?" is at the heart of the song. The characters in *Rent* live in a world fraught with crime and poverty, disease and death, homelessness and drug addiction. Their answer to the question was not about giving up or allowing themselves to be swallowed up by that world. Instead, they proudly proclaimed that the best response was to live as fully in the present moment as possible and to attach the greatest value to love:

How about love?

How about love?

How about love?

Measure in love

Seasons of love

Jonathan Larson wanted to celebrate and honor his friends and the community of which he was a part. As an artist, he understood the challenges creative individuals face in their struggle to support themselves, practice their art, and become recognized. "Seasons of Love" can be understood as Larson's message of hope and his affirmation of life.

Chapter 4

Long Live *Rent!*

Rent was not the first musical to feature a cast of youthful performers in a contemporary setting. Think *West Side Story* or *Hair*. *West Side Story* ran on Broadway from 1957–1959, and in 1961, the film version was released. The musical (inspired by William Shakespeare's late sixteenth-century tragedy *Romeo and Juliet*) concerns the turf rivalry between two New York City gangs—one white (the Jets), the other Puerto Rican (the Sharks). When Tony (a former Jet) falls in love with Maria (whose brother is leader of the Sharks), the tension escalates and builds toward a tragic ending.

The show's gritty urban drama, electrifying choreography, and soul-stirring songs, as well as the inclusion of Latino characters, steered musical theater in

Opposite: On the closing night of *Rent* in 2008, fans of the show left farewell messages.

a brand-new direction and led to the emergence of other youth-filled musicals like *Hair* and *Rent*.

The Legacy of *Rent*

Rent, like its predecessors, captured a particular time and place: New York's East Village in the early 90s, when young people lived in the shadow of AIDS and a pervasive drug culture. The times have changed. The Village has become gentrified. And a diagnosis of HIV is not necessarily a death sentence. But the search for love and community is never out of fashion, and artists still struggle to survive in a world that increasingly negates the value of art.

Though *Rent* may have become somewhat dated in its depiction of young bohemians striving for artistic purity, the musical represents a milestone in the history of Broadway theater. As one fan noted on a media blog: "Growing up in New York City, one of the first Broadway musicals I had ever seen was *Rent*. It was edgy, it was modern, and it had rock music—it was the coolest thing I had ever seen." Rock music, actors wearing clothes from used clothing stores or their own closets, a story that included homeless people, junkies, people who are HIV-positive, a set design without scene changes, and an artfully assembled tower of junk meant to symbolize a Christmas tree—these were some of the innovations in *Rent* that had critics raving and audiences lined up along the sidewalk outside the theater.

Rival gang members face off in a knife fight in *West Side Story*, a 1950s musical.

Lin-Manuel Miranda Follows in Larson's Footsteps

Jonathan Larson wanted *Rent* to forever change the way Broadway staged musicals. His central goal was to fuse pop/rock music with musical theater. There have been some worthy successors to *Rent*. One of the most outstanding shows to accomplish much the same is the Broadway smash hit *Hamilton*. When Lin-Manuel Miranda, the show's creator, was seventeen, he saw *Rent* for the first time. That experience inspired him to write musicals. Like Larson, he wanted to revitalize Broadway with popular music.

Miranda grew up in New York City as the son of immigrant parents from Puerto Rico and listened to rap and hip-hop through his teenage years. When writing the score for *Hamilton*, he succeeded in combining rap and hip-hop with a story about the life of Alexander Hamilton, one of America's Founding Fathers. Hamilton was the country's first treasury secretary as well as a hero of the American Revolution. He came here in 1774 as a poor immigrant from an island in the West Indies. In 2004, Miranda was reading a biography on Hamilton when he sensed a connection between the hip-hop rhythms he grew up with and the feelings expressed in the writings of the Founding Fathers, like Hamilton and Thomas Jefferson. According to writer Alisa Solomon, "Soon [Miranda] was working on a mixtape that mashed up the Founding Fathers with beat-boxing bruthas [brothers]." From this beginning, *Hamilton* was born. The show opened in August 2015 and, like *Rent*, has become a hugely successful Broadway show.

The Stars of *Rent* Continue to Shine

Actors in the Broadway production of *Rent* have come and gone throughout the show's twelve-year run from 1996 until it closed in 2008. But the original cast holds a special place in the hearts of diehard fans. The experience of performing in *Rent* enabled these actors to pursue successful careers not only in theater but in television and film as well. Below is a table showing the eight principal roles and the actors who played them:

ROLE	ACTOR
Mark Cohen (filmmaker)	Anthony Rapp
Roger Davis (musician)	Adam Pascal
Benjamin Coffin III ("Benny," the landlord)	Taye Diggs
Mimi Marquez (exotic dancer)	Daphne Rubin-Vega
Maureen Johnson (performance artist)	Idina Menzel
Joanne Jefferson (lawyer and Maureen's girlfriend)	Fredi Walker
Angel Dumott Shunard (street musician)	Wilson Jermaine Heredia
Tom Collins (philosophy professor and Angel's lover)	Jesse L. Martin

After leaving *Rent*, Anthony Rapp (Mark) performed in the musical *You're a Good Man, Charlie Brown*. He has also appeared in movies and television shows, and he wrote a book about his experience in *Rent* called *Without You:*

Original cast member Anthony Rapp (Mark) belts out a song on ABC's *Good Morning America* in 2008.

A Memoir of Love, Loss, and the Musical Rent. Rapp also starred in the Broadway musical *If/Then* with fellow *Rent* star Idina Menzel.

Adam Pascal (Roger) had no acting experience when he was cast in *Rent*. But he could sing and play guitar, and he had his own band, Mute. His acting career took off after his stint in *Rent*. He performed in several musicals, including *Elton John, Studio 54,* and *Aida*. Adam reprised his role in the film version of *Rent*, released in 2005. In addition to performing, he has started a gluten-free food company with his wife.

Taye Diggs (Benny) went on to star in the Broadway musical *Chicago* and in many TV series including *Murder in the First*, which was cancelled in 2016 after three seasons. Diggs also starred in another musical, *Hedwig and the Angry Inch*.

Daphne Rubin-Vega (Mimi) has performed in a number of Broadway revivals, including *The Rocky Horror Picture Show* and *Les Misérables*. She appeared in the 2008 film *Sex and the City* and in the second season of the TV series *Smash*, which ran from 2012–2013.

Idina Menzel (Maureen) has enjoyed great success since appearing in *Rent*. She won a Tony Award for her work in *Wicked*, the Broadway musical in which she originated the part of Elphaba. She's also acted in the TV show *Glee* and provided the voice of Queen Elsa in the animated Disney film *Frozen*.

After her role as Joanne in *Rent*, Fredi Walker continued to star in Broadway musicals, like *The Lion King*, *Little Shop of Horrors* and *The Buddy Holly Story*. She also appeared in the long-running TV series *Law and Order*.

Wilson Jermaine Heredia (Angel) won the 1996 Tony and Drama Desk Awards for Best Featured Actor in a Musical for his performance in *Rent*. A Brooklyn native, he had wanted to pursue a career in advertising, but the need to express himself eventually won out. So he became an actor. He reprised the role of Angel in the movie version of *Rent* and starred on Broadway in the musical *La Cage aux Folles*. Inspired by his musically talented parents, Wilson has choreographed and danced in a number of music videos.

Jesse L. Martin (Collins) has become a familiar face on television since appearing in *Rent*. His TV credits include roles in *One Life to Live, Guiding Light,* and *Law and Order*. In addition to performing in regional theaters, he has appeared on Broadway in *Timon of Athens* and *The Government Inspector*. As of 2017, Jesse stars as Detective Joe West in the TV show *The Flash*.

Rent, in Film and Audio

In 2005, the film version of *Rent* was released. With the exceptions of Daphne Rubin-Vega (Mimi) and Fredi Walker (Joanne), the original 1996 Broadway cast reprised their roles in the movie. Rosario Dawson was given the role of Mimi, and Tracie Thoms was cast as Joanne. At the time of the movie's production, Rubin-Vega was pregnant, and Walker felt she was too old to continue playing the part of Joanne.

The original cast also recorded all the songs from the musical. The recording was produced by DreamWorks and released on August 27, 1996. It has sold more than two million copies.

The Show Must Go On ... and On and On ...

In 1996 and 1997, there were two highly successful North American tours of *Rent*. Both were named after two of the main characters. The Angel Tour opened on November 5, 1996 and closed on September 5, 1999. The Benny Tour opened on September 16, 1997 and closed on July 15,

The cast of the movie version of *Rent* included performers from the original Broadway musical.

2001. The show has been performed in at least twenty-one different languages and in cities around the world. In 2008, high school theater groups around the country were able to secure the rights to perform an adaptation of the musical. The *Rent School Edition* retains the basic plot. However, the language has been modified somewhat and one song—"Contact"—was eliminated. Otherwise, it keeps the action focused on a group of friends and artists in the 1990s confronting the AIDS epidemic, poverty, and drug addiction.

To celebrate the tenth anniversary of *Rent* in 2006, the original cast reunited for a one-night-only performance at the theater where it all began. The event was well attended and raised over two million dollars for the Jonathan Larson Performing Arts Foundation, the New York Theatre Workshop, and Friends in Deed, a nonprofit resource center

RENT'S INFLUENCE
Lin-Manuel Miranda, the star and creator of *Hamilton*, was not the only member of the cast greatly influenced by *Rent*. So was Leslie Odom Jr., who originated the role of Aaron Burr in the musical. Odom recalls that when he was a kid, the experience of seeing *Rent* opened his heart and senses for the first time.

originally organized in 1991 for people with life-threatening diseases like AIDS.

Rent may have ended its Broadway run in 2008, but the show was far from over. The final performance was filmed live in high-definition at the Nederlander Theatre on September 7. The end of the film features a spirited gathering of the original cast with the actors in the closing performance.

And on September 12, 2016, the twentieth anniversary national tour of *Rent* held its first performance in Bloomington, Indiana. Slated to run into 2018, the tour consists of mostly one-night stands in different cities. The cast is made up of a new generation of actors in their twenties. Although the production stays pretty close to the original staging, there are some minor changes in the lighting and some of the choreography. The show's original costumer, choreographer, and musical director are on hand as part of the creative team.

LONGEST RUNNING SHOWS ON BROADWAY

RANK	SHOW	PERFORMANCES
1	*The Phantom of the Opera* *	12,326
2	*Chicago* *	8,651
3	*The Lion King* *	8,254
4	*Cats*	7,485
5	*Les Misérables*	6,680
6	*A Chorus Line*	6,137
7	*Oh! Calcutta!*	5,959
8	*Wicked**	5,787
9	*Mamma Mia!*	5,758
10	*Beauty and the Beast*	5,461
11	*Rent*	5,123
12	*Jersey Boys*	4,642

* Still running

Source: Internet Broadway Database

Glossary

ACRONYM An abbreviation formed from the initial letters of other words.

ALTRUISTIC Unselfish, charitable.

ANEURYSM An abnormal enlargement of an artery caused by a weakness in its wall.

AUTHENTICITY True, believable; characters that lack authenticity strike the audience as fake, implausible.

BABY BOOMER Someone born between 1945 and the late 1960s, though an "end date" of 1964 is sometimes used.

BOURGEOIS Refers to the characteristics of the middle class. "Bourgeois values" refers to perceived materialistic values or conventional attitudes and is typically a criticism.

CAPITALISM An economic and political system in which trade and industry are controlled, for profit, by private owners.

CHOPS Skill or excellence in a field or activity, such as acting or playing an instrument.

CRITIQUE To evaluate or analyze something—in this case, a dress rehearsal.

DEMOGRAPHIC A particular sector of a population, such as teens.

DESTITUTE Not having the necessities of life, such as a healthy place to live and adequate food.

GARRET A room at the top of a house, just under the roof, much like an attic.

HARDSCRABBLE Requiring hard work and struggle that typically provides little in return.

LEGACY Something which is transmitted by a predecessor. In *Rent*, Roger wants to create a memorable song as his legacy.

MILIEU A physical or social setting.

MILLENNIUM A period of one thousand years. The twenty-first century, which began January 1, 2001, is the first century of the third millennium.

MUSICAL IDIOM A style of music for a particular period, such as pop, rock, jazz, blues.

PREVIEW A performance in advance of the official opening of a show that provides an opportunity for corrections or improvements before the critics are invited to watch.

SEMINAL A work—such as the musical *Hair* and later the musical *Rent*—that is strongly influential. An event, moment, or figure can also be considered seminal.

STATUS QUO The existing state; how things are right now.

SUNG-THROUGH A musical (also, a musical film or opera) that has no spoken dialogue, with the possible exception of some spoken lines in the lyrics.

SYNTHESIZER An electronic musical instrument, typically operated by a keyboard.

TRAJECTORY A path or a line of development. In this use, it applies to an evolving relationship.

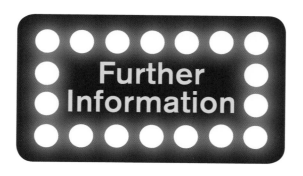

Further Information

BOOKS

Hodges, Drew. *On Broadway: From Rent to Revolution.* New York: Rizzoli, 2016.

Jones, John Bush. *Our Musicals, Ourselves: A Social History of the American Musical Theatre.* New Hampshire: Brandeis University Press, 2003.

McDonnell, Evelyn, and Katherine Silberger, eds. *Rent.* New York: Rob Weisbach Books, 1997.

Musicals: The Definitive Illustrated Story. New York: DK Publishing, 2015.

Rapp, Anthony. *Without You: A Memoir of Love, Loss, and the Musical* Rent. New York: Simon & Schuster, 2006.

Viertel, Jack. *The Secret Life of the American Musical: How Broadway Shows are Built.* New York: Sarah Crichton Books, 2016.

WEBSITES

La Bohème: Opera by Puccini

https://www.britannica.com/topic/La-Boheme-opera-by-Puccini

This comprehensive essay provides background and context, cast, and vocal parts, as well as a story summary.

Music Theater International: *Rent*

http://www.mtishows.com/rent

This company offers (for a fee) a version of *Rent* suitable for school productions.

VIDEOS

"6 Brilliant Moments—and Even More Crazy Facts— From the Incredible Rent Reunion."

http://www.playbill.com/article/6-brilliant-moments-and-even-more-crazy-facts-from-the-incredible-rent-reunion-com-381798

Embedded in this article is a twelve-minute video featuring some of the original stars of the show discussing their experiences.

Rent Live on Broadway, 2008

https://www.youtube.com/watch?v=Lo8CmwIKiDw

The entire show has been posted to YouTube.

Rent, the Musical, "Light My Candle"

https://www.youtube.com/watch?v=T05DzTH1_2E

Renée Elise Goldsberry, who won a Tony for her role as Angelica Schuyler in Hamilton, faces off against Will Chase in this performance.

Rent, the Musical, "Seasons of Love"

https://www.youtube.com/watch?v=ZLjFGwivFtU

A live performance of *Rent*'s most popular song.

ONLINE ARTICLES

Blake, Meredith. "*How to Survive a Plague* revisits the early days of AIDS epidemic." *Los Angeles Times*, February 20, 2013. http://articles.latimes.com/2013/feb/20/entertainment/la-et-mn-how-to-survive-a-plague-david-france-20130224.

Cantoni, Linda, and Betsy Schwarm. "La Boheme (Opera by Puccini)." Encyclopaedia Britannica. Accessed October 5, 2017. https://www.britannica.com/topic/La-Boheme-opera-by-Puccini.

Couillard, Lucie. "Where the Original Cast of the Broadway Musical *Rent* is Now." *New York Daily News*, December 28, 2015. http://www.nydailynews.com/entertainment/theater-arts/cast-rent-article-1.2478997.

Fierberg, Ruthie. "6 Brilliant Moments—and Even More Crazy Facts—from the Incredible *Rent* Reunion." *Playbill*, January 23, 2016. http://www.playbill.com/article/6-brilliant-moments-and-even-more-crazy-facts-from-the-incredible-rent-reunion-com-381798.

Flynn, Rosalind. "*Rent*: A Full Length Rock Musical by Jonathan Larson." ThoughtCo, June 23, 2016. https://www.thoughtco.com/rent-4056996

Gioia, Michael. "The Creation of *Rent* – How Jonathan Larson Transformed an Idea into a Groundbreaking Musical." *Playbill*, February 5, 2016. http://www.playbill.com/article/the-creation-of-rent-how-jonathan-larson-transformed-an-idea-into-a-groundbreaking-musical.

Hopkins, Kate. "The Satirical Stories that Inspired *La Bohème*." Royal Opera House website, July 12, 2014. http://www.roh.org.uk/news/the-satirical-stories-that-inspired-la-boheme

Houfek, Susanne. "A Real Bohemian Explores Her Roots and Finds a Unique Culture Intact Within the Term Bohemian." *Realize*. Accessed October 5, 2017. http://realizemagazine.com/content/real-bohemian-explores-her-roots

"*La Boheme*." The France of Victor Hugo: Bohemianism and Counter-Culture. Accessed September 18, 2017. https://www.mtholyoke.edu/courses/rschwart/hist255/bohem/tlaboheme.html

Leland, John. "The East Village, in the 1980s and Looking Back." *New York Times*, December 26, 2014. https://www.nytimes.com/2014/12/28/nyregion/the-east-village-in-the-1980s-and-looking-back.html?mcubz=3#.

Lipsky, David. "Jonathan Larson & *Rent*'s History." Accessed September 20, 2017. http://www.angelfire.com/in2/everythingisrent/jon.html.

Miller, Scott. "Inside *Rent*." Excerpt from *Rebels with Applause: Broadway's Groundbreaking Musicals*. New Hampshire: Heinemann Drama, 2001. http://www.newlinetheatre.com/rentchapter.html.

Milzoff, Rebecca. "*Rent*: The Oral History." Vulture, Accessed September 25, 2017. http://www.vulture.com/2016/04/rent-oral-history-c-v-r.html.

Neal, Dyana. "The Bohemian Life According to Henri Murger (1822-1861)." WBJC.com. Accessed September 25, 2017. http://www.wbjc.com/the-bohemian-life.

Phillips, Tazi. "See vintage photos of the East Village in the 1980s." *Time Out: New York*, August 27, 2015. https://www.timeout.com/newyork/things-to-do/see-vintage-photos-of-the-east-village-in-the-1980s.

"*Rent* by Jonathan Larson." Broadway Musical Home. Accessed September 19, 2017. http://broadwaymusicalhome.com/shows/rent.htm

Solomon, Serena. "HIV/AIDS-Ravaged East Village Music Scene Focus of Documentary." DNAInfo.com, December 1, 2011. https://www.dnainfo.com/new-york/20111201/lower-east-side-east-village/hivaidsravaged-east-village-music-scene-focus-of-documentary

Towers, Andrea, and Dana Rose Falcone. "*Rent* turns 20: Ranking All the Musical's Songs." *Entertainment Weekly*, January 26, 2016. http://ew.com/article/2016/01/26/rent-song-rankings-20-year-anniversary.

Varley, Eddie. "Tracie Thoms: *Rent*'s 'Dream Girl.'" BroadwayWorld.com, August 17, 2008. https://www.broadwayworld.com/article/Tracie-Thoms-RENTs-Dream-Girl-20080817

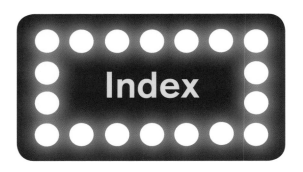

Index

Page numbers in **boldface** are illustrations.

About the Author

GEORGE CAPACCIO once worked as the creative arts director for a summer camp in the Berkshires of Massachusetts. One of his responsibilities was to direct a musical show with the campers. He had never in his life directed a musical, or any type of show for that matter. But that didn't stop him. He chose the romantic comedy *The Fantasticks*. The experience of putting on a play—especially one with music— was a life-changing experience for George and inspired him to become a theater artist.